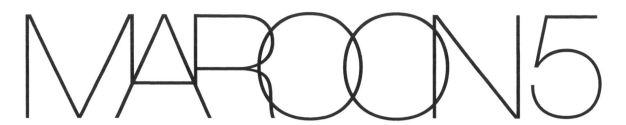

# MAROON 5

## SONGS**ABOUT**JANE

T0053219

DISTRIBUTED BY

HAL•LEONARD®
CORPORATION

7777 W. BLUEMOUND RD. P.O. BOX 13819 MILWAUKEE, WI 53213

# HARDER TO BREATHE

WORDS & MUSIC BY ADAM LEVINE, JAMES VALENTINE,
JESSE CARMICHAEL, MICKEY MADDEN & RYAN DUSICK

you'll un - der - stand what I mean____ when I say____ there's no way____ we're gon - na give up.____ And like a lit - tle girl cries____ in the face____ of a mon - ster that lives____ in her dreams.____ Is there a - ny - one out____ there 'cause it's get - ting hard -

*Drums*

# THIS LOVE

**WORDS & MUSIC BY ADAM LEVINE, JAMES VALENTINE,
JESSE CARMICHAEL, MICKEY MADDEN & RYAN DUSICK**

1. I was so high I did not re-cog-nise the fire burn-ing
2. I tried my best to feed her ap-pe-tite, to keep her com - ing

I'll fix___ these bro - ken things,___ re - pair___ your bro - ken wings

and make___ sure ev - 'ry - thing's___ al - right.

My pres - sure on___ your hips,___ oh, sink - ing___ my fing - er tips,___ in - to

ev - 'ry inch of you___ be - cause I know___ that's what___ you want___ me to___ do.

# SHIVER

WORDS & MUSIC BY ADAM LEVINE, JAMES VALENTINE,
JESSE CARMICHAEL, MICKEY MADDEN & RYAN DUSICK

1. You build me up, you knock me down,
2. Im-mo-bil-ized by the thought of you.

to your heart, so I guess I'd bet-ter find a new way in.

I shi-ver when I hear your name, think a-bout you but it's

not the same. I won't be sa-tis-fied till I'm un-der your

skin.

*Guitar*

find a\_\_\_\_ new way in.    I\_\_\_\_ shi - ver when I

hear your\_\_\_\_ name,    think a - bout you but it's

not the\_\_\_\_ same.    I won't be sa - tis - fied till I'm un - der your

**1.**

skin.    Yeah,\_ yeah,\_ yeah!

**2.**

skin.    Yeah,\_ yeah,\_ yeah!\_

# SHE WILL BE LOVED

WORDS & MUSIC BY ADAM LEVINE, JAMES VALENTINE,
JESSE CARMICHAEL, MICKEY MADDEN & RYAN DUSICK

Cm                 B♭7            E♭sus²

- how I___ want more.___
___ a - ny - time you want.___

I don't mind spend - ing

B♭sus⁴          Cm¹¹          B♭sus⁴

ev - e - ry day___ out on your cor - ner in the pour - ing___ rain.___

E♭sus²          B♭sus⁴          Cm¹¹

Look for the girl with the bro - ken smile,___ ask her if she wants to

A♭add9          E♭sus²          B♭sus⁴

stay a - while. And she will___ be loved,___ and she will___

# TANGLED

WORDS & MUSIC BY ADAM LEVINE, JAMES VALENTINE,
JESSE CARMICHAEL, MICKEY MADDEN & RYAN DUSICK

of re - grets for all the things that I have done and said. And

**Am**

I You're just don't know an in - no - cent, if it -'ll ev - er be O. a help - less vic - tim of a

**F**

**E⁵**  **Am**

K. to show my face a - round here. spi - ders web and I'm an in - sect,

**F**  **E⁵**  **Fmaj⁷**

Some - times I won - der if I dis - ap - pear, would you ev - er turn go - ing af - ter a - ny - thing that I can get. So you bet - ter turn

# THE SUN

### WORDS & MUSIC BY ADAM LEVINE, JAMES VALENTINE, JESSE CARMICHAEL, MICKEY MADDEN & RYAN DUSICK

1. Aft - er school,_____ walk - ing home, fresh dirt un - der my fing -
2. Mov - ing on_____ down my street, I see peo - ple I won't ev -

things ain't how\_\_ they used\_\_ to be.\_\_ She said the bat - tle's al - most won\_\_

\_\_ and we're on - ly sev - en miles\_\_ from the sun.\_\_

*To Coda*

Oh,_____ yeah.\_\_

**1.**

**2.** \_\_ from the sun.\_\_

# MUST GET OUT

WORDS & MUSIC BY ADAM LEVINE, JAMES VALENTINE,
JESSE CARMICHAEL, MICKEY MADDEN & RYAN DUSICK

1. I've been the nee - dle and___
2. "This is not___ good - bye"___

Try to guide_ me in_ the right_ di - rec - tion._

Mak - ing use_ of all_ this time,_ keep - ing ev - 'ry - thing in - side,_

close my eyes_ and lis - ten to_ you cry._

I'm lift - ing you up,_ I'm let - ting you down,_ I'm dan - cing till dawn_

I'm fool - ing a - round.___ I'm not giv - ing up,___ I'm mak - ing your love.__

This ci - ty's made us cra - zy and__ we must get__ out.___ Oh,___

___ yeah,_____ oh.

There's on - ly so__ much I__ can do_____ for you.

# SUNDAY MORNING

### WORDS & MUSIC BY ADAM LEVINE, JAMES VALENTINE, JESSE CARMICHAEL, MICKEY MADDEN & RYAN DUSICK

Yeah.

1. Sun - day morn - ing, rain is fall - ing.
2. Fing - ers trace your ev - 'ry out - line.

Steal some cov - ers, share some skin.
Paint a pic - ture with my hands.

Clouds are shroud - ing us in mo - ments un - for - get - ta - ble. You twist
Back and forth we sway like branch - es in a storm. Change the wea -

*1° only*

_ to fit the mould that I am in. But things
- ther, still to - ge - ther when it ends.

44

# SECRET

WORDS & MUSIC BY ADAM LEVINE, JAMES VALENTINE,
JESSE CARMICHAEL, MICKEY MADDEN & RYAN DUSICK

Watch the sun - rise,_____ say your good - byes,_____ off

51

# NOT COMING HOME

WORDS & MUSIC BY ADAM LEVINE, JAMES VALENTINE,
JESSE CARMICHAEL, MICKEY MADDEN & RYAN DUSICK

1. When you re - fuse___ me you con - fuse___ me.___
2. You do not know___ how much this hurts___ me,___

What makes you think I'll let you in a - gain?___
to say these things that I want to say but have to say them a - ny - way.

Think a - gain___ my friend.     Go on, mis - use___ me and a -
                                I would do a - ny - thing to end

- buse me.___                I'll come out
your suf - fer - ing.        But you would

strong - er in the end.
ra - ther walk a - way.

**A**     **C♯m/B**     **C♯m/C**

Does it make you sad to find your - self a - lone?

**C♯m**     **A**     **C♯m/B**

Does it make you mad to

**C♯m/C**     **C♯m**     **A**

find that I have grown? Bet it hurts

56

# THROUGH WITH YOU

### WORDS & MUSIC BY ADAM LEVINE, JAMES VALENTINE, JESSE CARMICHAEL, MICKEY MADDEN & RYAN DUSICK

and that's not how things were sup - posed to be.

You take my hand just to give it back,— no oth - er lov - er has

ev - er done that. Do you re - mem - ber the way we used to melt, do you re -

-mem - ber how it felt when I touched you? Oh, 'cause I re - mem - ber ve - ry

back to me — and that's not how things were sup-
have so much, a sim-ple love with a

-posed to be. You take my hand just to
com-plex touch. And there is no-thing you can

**1, 3.**
give it back,— no oth-er lov-er has ev-er done that.——
say or do.— I

**2, 4.**
N.C. *To Coda* ⊕
called to let you know I'm through with you. Oh.——

*Drums*

know I'm through. I called to let you know I'm through. I called to let you

know I'm through with you. (I ain't ev-er com-ing back to you.)

# SWEETEST GOODBYE

WORDS & MUSIC BY ADAM LEVINE, JAMES VALENTINE,
JESSE CARMICHAEL, MICKEY MADDEN & RYAN DUSICK

stretched arms,__ op - en hearts.__ And if it nev - er ends then when__ do we__ start?__
rhy - thm of the rain__ that drops__ and co - in - cides with the beat - ing of__ my

heart. } I'll nev - er leave you be - hind____ or treat you un - kind.__

I know you un - der - stand.____ Oh,__ oh.__

And with a tear in my eye_____ give me the sweet - est good - bye__

that I ev - er did re - ceive.

Push - ing for - ward and arch - ing back.

*Instrumental to fade*

Bring me clo - ser to heart at - tack.

Say good - bye and just fly a - way.

8/05 (55742)